MUCH LEFT UNSAID

MUCH LEFT UNSAID

Finola Scott

Poems

RED SQUIRREL PRESS

First published in 2019 by Red Squirrel Press
36 Elphinstone Crescent
Biggar
South Lanarkshire
ML12 6GU
www.redsquirrelpress.com

Edited by Elizabeth Rimmer
www.burnedthumb.co.uk

Typesetting and design by Gerry Cambridge
e:gerry.cambridge@btinternet.com

Copyright © Finola Scott 2019

The right of Finola Scott to be identified as the author of this work has been asserted by her in accordance with Section 77 of the Copyright, Designs and Patents Act 1988.

All rights reserved.

A CIP catalogue record is available from the British Library.

ISBN: 978 1 910437 86 5

Red Squirrel Press is committed to a sustainable future. This book is printed in Scotland by Love & Humphries using Forest Stewardship Council certified paper.
www.loveandprint.co.uk

With love to those who support, encourage and make me laugh

Contents

Acrobat • 9
Loads • 10
Pilgrimage • 11
Arranged • 12
Breakfast of champions • 13
The first time • 14
Teguise, Lanzarote 1618 • 15
Camino • 16
Riding the marches • 17
Planes over Guernica • 18
Ortha-pheamainn • 19
Much left unsaid • 20
Using dad's binoculars • 21
Arctic colour chart • 22
Walk on the wild side • 23
Cardowan Colliery, North Lanarkshire • 24
Air and sound • 25
Matryoshka dolls • 26
Speed trials, Hogganfield Loch • 27
All sheets to the wind • 28

Acknowledgments • 31
A NOTE ON THE TYPE • 32

Acrobat

I teeter downhill nearly head over heels
tipped by your tumbling weight.

No safety net, Glasgow spreads below.
The lollipop lady opens arms wide.

The steep street's a tight-rope,
two hearts dance on this high wire,

my blood a memory in your veins.
Upright uptight I fight gravity's pull,

coiled you wrestle the waxing moon.
On tiptoe I balance our hopes

let love steady our way.

Loads

The rush in late summer sun
        to peg out washing
Faded duvet   partner-less   pillowcase
   single sheets
       at careless intervals

recall other loads. Endless
squares   of bleached towelling
   sang   of milky skin   topped and tailed
                       in unison
Tiny mittens   vests   gowns
      clothes   for changelings
Dolly pegs   prance along   tight
   ropes of tomorrow

This evening's breeze   carries   a chill

Pilgrimage

Head south, out of Glasgow, follow signs Eaglesham, Fenwick,
   out away.
Don't stop at the tea room.
      Catch the sun.

Turn off, keep turning off. It's the moor road you need. In the
   shadow of Balygeoch
is a car-park. It'll be busy.
      That's not the one.

The road gets narrower, air colder, sounds clearer, lapwing
   plentiful, cries plaintive.
The sky is wide and high. The smell of coconut gorse.
      You'd better wear wellies.

Out across the marsh, over barbed wire, through reed beds.
   Yellow flags of iris signal,
bog cotton flutters. The land turns its back and midges welcome you.
      Almost there.

Arranged

after *Paper Shoes*, sculpture by Isabell Buenz

Mute as mum
   hauls the corset   hooks her
in unsullied the dress a heavy fall
   slithers   unresisting
ghost-silk parcels flesh.
  Her fate gauze-veiled
cloaked   she steps up
   into parchment shoes
        teeters
feet-bound   path set.
  Tries to find wriggle room
toes bruise   against the white pebble
her mother placed there.

Breakfast of champions

Sharing this moment
our afterwards meal
padding barefoot in your
emperor dressing gown
I'm undone

Whistling
you rule your kitchen kingdom
with chopping board & sureness
Bulging bags spill
asparagus   smoked salmon
cantaloupe   peaches
You froth eggs & hearts
in a spicy flourish
leftovers tossed away,
you command *Ready. Now.*

My mornings alone are calm
I stir the porridge
wi a guid plain spurtle
as hungry foxes stalk my lawn.

The first time

Two girls not yet women, sprawl
on the living room carpet.
The summer night thickens, grainy
images on the tv shimmer.

The girls share attention between
the familiar suburban sky and the screen.
Applause swells in Houston as climax approaches.
On the turntable, Jagger brags
of Honky Tonk Women.

No man on either Moon,
not yet. Luna spins, watches.
She can move oceans, but cannot
evade the metal men.
The moment. They land, jump
stamp. Her skin bruises

Teguise, Lanzarote 1619

Pirates enter on a day thick with storms.
The shutters are snicked too late,
the fincas barred in vain. Heavy cloud
tricks the watchers while sails wait furled
at the coast. Death is here, on the cobbles.
The raiders twist in smooth as corkscrews.
Flagstones shine sangre slippy with the spilt
lives of sons, uncles, friends. Hidden away
Juana thinks of the old man her father
has chosen for her groom.

The women jostle to peer through slits
in the fortress that squats on the shoulder
of the volcano. The ground shudders to the whack
and crack of bones in the town below. Echoing
oaths rebound in courtyards. Maria and Fayna
are puzzled by the blue eyes, bear-fierce beards,
careless laughter of the marauders hurtling in.
Juana's mother pushes her into the shadows,
orders her to cover her ebony hair, hide her
jewels. But Juana stands on tiptoe to marvel
at the grit and spit of lava on their lips.

Camino

Here I am bumflapping
at the edge again.

The crumpled gown refuses
to close, unpainted toes dangle.

Check my bag—phone, bruised
antenatal card.

I think of ribbons tied to branches,
scallop shells pinned to cloaks,

reflect on heartache, incubators.
Bring the card to my lips.

Riding the marches

If I had thought, taken a sliver of time,
I'd have checked my soft boundaries.
Ridden them regular, cut a sod of turf,
nailed a herring to a bannock,
minded my back.
But I didn't hear moss sneak and stretch.
Didn't see larks' tongues wag.
Dark vigilance or weary watching might
have spared me wounds.
Walls, hedges encroached unseen.
Markers moved in midnight hush,
rocks lured by deceitful streams.
Unguarded my safety shrank as the vixen sang.
Masked strangers, marauders, came
trusted at my door, as friends not foe.
Too late for cavalcades or queens.

Planes over Guernica

Lanzarote, Spring 1937

The artist hides in a cave
doesn't sketch bison hunts.
His feet crackle on black gravel,
rust red rock above his head.

He goes where lava
sizzled into sea, hauls
strange fish from nooks, catches
scent of rosemary, scuffle of lizards.
A rabbit listens for stoats, a yellow butterfly
in a spider's web.

He creeps like a cloud over
the blistered isle, sits in star dark,
tastes wind from Africa,
waits for Franco to finish.

Ortha-fheamainn

Seaweed charm

swathes of storm-beached weed
knit themselves
 to pass the time
  cast on strands
   brown- black *laminaria hyperborea* copper
    fucus vesiculosus slub bladderwrack
     emerald silk sea lettuce khaki ochre
    cream purple ruby *palmaria palmata*
   cast off
   slippy shawls
skeins of a raddled past

hanks loaded on carts
horsehauled creel carried
fieldspread furrows loaded
strands leech sweet into tatties
tangled ravelled on skerries
this kelp forest lies furled
bundle-snarled.

Much left unsaid

Deep night shifts, shudders.
His defiant lungs creak, cracking silence.
The guardian lamp keeps
scattered focus sharp.

Rafters sigh with burdens. Generations
of memories lie folded in tissue. The room
waits for a steady rhythm, holds stale breath.
Outside neon street lights flicker flash.

His bedroom's now a Cabinet of Curiosities,
bedside table a pharmaceutical clutter,
hunched in the corner, the arachnid zimmer.
Cuff links and War medals rest redundant.

Soft white cotton slides on mottled skin.
Bed rails jangle as chicken-bone knuckles
grasp in the dark. His skeletal head swivels
seeking the amethyst gift-wrapped hyacinths.

I hold his hand, begin to sing.

Using dad's binoculars

Hefting his knowledge in their weight,
I note beak shapes, flight patterns,
scan bird-scratchings in tidal mud.
Listen.
The air is swollen with song but I know
identification is often luck.
A beginner again, in shifting light I observe
the whirling acrobats, their glitterback gloss,
smell the breath of garrulous gulls. Always
I try to master the accumulation of wings.

Arctic colour chart

opaque sky   flickerglows to east
   flatline   colourwashed
icebleached   only blue   sky sea sky   frozenfingers
  forgetmenot   blood-clotted veins   cornflower   blue
    timecrushed ice   water worn   airless
         bubbleless   compressed
   eua de nile   aquamarine   gleams

    skyline fountains   white spume
  skua   in summer glut   gannet
creamwinged   peachtinged   tuck
       wings to arrows   plunge
  all pythagorean angles   bisect
    squeezed glacierwater   melting
Melville whales   tease and tempt   flick
       flack   twofingered tails   at tourists.

Walk on the wild side

The Wadden Sea Netherlands

This is no sea. Here,
folk are Sunday strollers
lugworm squishers,
periwinkle prodders.

My sea batters and beats,
ravages coasts, gouges caves
rips cliffs, beaches selkies,
press-gangs locals.

This, this is a polished pond,
a made-up mirror of mercury
mud and shifting wetland,
of gullies and salt marshes.

When the brackish mire deepens
the weak ride tractors back,
as curlews unfurl and flee
and seals pass judgement
on this soft lipped coast.

Cardowan Colliery, North Lanarkshire

My rubble-full garden's no use for digging,
I don't dare go deep. At times I hear canaries
cheep for breath, bogies rattle rails, bent men
cough for sunlight at end of days.

In the church car park, traffic in shifts
charts the days. Flower Arranging, Choir Practice.
Wedding-hatted women, lads in fierce pride kilts.
Floodlights keep the dark in its place.

Tarmac over pit-propped caverns, shaky hollows,
greedy snaking tunnels. The dead recorded
in the new estate roads where salaried men drive home,
hands soft and clean, music playing.

The earth remembers.

Air and sound

1 *La Gomera, Canary Isles*

Ravine separated, the lovers whistle longing.
Lips craving kisses send soft touches, promises
of tomorrows. Love-letter notes ripple misted valleys.
On this rock at Africa's edge, neighbours
catch heart-piercing chords, hear harmony.

2 *Kirkmichael, Ayrshire*

I work my brother's ordered garden,
try to untangle the geometry of song, the pitch of love.
Grown, we remember decoding Mum's bright warble
that called us from play. From the house roof, a mavis
declares sunset. Finches tune their lust.

Matryoshka dolls

We sit book ended
on the sofa
cooried close
my daughter and I

Feel Mum, swollen she turns
towards me, her belly
a ripening pod.

Inside my child, cells divide
  and divide.
Curled, crouched, coiled
my child fuses and swells.

I cradle her cocoon
and feel in my daughter,
her daughter dance beneath my hands
practising for later.

I cup once familiar flesh
hold another's foot curve, heart.
Practise.

Speed trials Hogganfield Loch

Hooking the wind, they rush
whoosh, claim the space, name it.
Joggers glare, miss beats, consider
evasive action.

Speed isn't all. Style counts.
The grace of velocity, the angle of curve,
strategy of deceleration. Celebration
of corners.

Swans, Granny!

True to their name the birds whoop
as they swoop the loch.
In a linen-sheeted glide,
they're down, feet flapping water.

My wee ones brace, stabiliser balanced.
Pink helmets cradle
baby-bird bones. No steadying
hand at their backs.

All sheets to the wind

When it's time, flap me, wrap me
to sleep, in silk, all printed with travels
and you. Skin unsullied, hair
story-booked, I'll dream drift
on a different curve. My toes will tingle-grip
all the sand, all the puddles we plashed.

Tuck me tight in map-memories
contoured streets, frescoes and freesias.
Soothe me
anchorless liminal.
Set me full sail.

Acknowledgements

Many of these poems have been previously published:

An earlier version of 'Acrobat', *Shorelines, Anthology of Federation of Writers,* 2012.
'Pilgrimage', The Ofi Press, 2015.
'Breakfast of champions', *Raum* Magazine, 2015.
'Teguise, Lanzarote, 1618, *The Blue Nib*, 2018.
A version of 'Camino', *The Blue Nib*, 2017.
'Planes over Guernica', *Ink, Sweat and Tears*, 2018.
'Ortha-pheamainn', *Coast to Coast*, 2019.
'Much left unsaid', *Mother's Milk Books Prize Winners' Anthology 2015, The Blue Nib Chapbook*, 2018.
'Using dad's binoculars', *Firth*, Issue 1, 2018.
'Arctic colour chart', *Coast to Coast*, 2017.
'Walk on the wild side', *Not A Drop Anthology,* Beautiful Dragons Press, 2016.
'Matryoshka dolls', *Bonnie's Crew Anthology*, 2018.
'Speed trials, Hogganfield Loch', *Atrium*, 2019.
'All sheets to the wind', The Ofi Press, 2018.

A NOTE ON THE TYPE

This pamphlet is set in Foundry Wilson, a redrawing of a 1760 font from Scottish type founder Alexander Wilson (1714–1786), a polymath who from 1760 to 1786 was the University of Glasgow's first Regius Professor of Astronomy. Many of Wilson's typefaces were produced exclusively for the Foulis brothers' classics published by Glasgow University Press. Foundry Wilson is a highly distinctive and robust serif typeface which functions excellently in a digital environment.